ISAIAH

God's Help Is on the Way

Marilyn Kunz
& Catherine Schell

13 Discussions for Group Bible Study

Neighborhood Bible Studies Publishers
Dobbs Ferry, NY

neighborhood bible studies

GROUP PARTICIPANTS

Name	Address	Phone Number

Scripture quotations, unless otherwise indicated, are taken from the HOLY BIBLE, NEW INTERNATIONAL VERSION®. Copyright © 1973, 1978, 1984 by International Bible Society. Used by permission of Zondervan Publishing House. All rights reserved.

All rights reserved. No part of this book may be reproduced or transmitted in any form or by any means, electronic or mechanical, including photocopying, recording, or any information storage and retrieval system without written permission from Neighborhood Bible Studies, 56 Main Street, Dobbs Ferry, New York, 10522; 1-800-369-0307; nbstudies@aol.com.

Copyright ©2002 by Marilyn Kunz and Catherine Schell

ISBN 1-880266-41-5
First printing November 2002
Printed in the United States of America
Cover photo by Fran Goodrich

Contents

How To Use this Discussion Guide

INTRODUCTION to Isaiah

Discussion 1   *Isaiah 6—8*
CALLED TO SERVE

Discussion 2   *Isaiah 9—12*
WARNINGS AND JOYOUS PROMISES

SUMMARY OF ISAIAH 13—23

Discussion 3   *Isaiah 24—27*
PUNISHMENT AND PRAISE, PROMISE OF VICTORY

Discussion 4   *Isaiah 28*
PROUD CROWN OR CROWN OF GLORY

Discussion 5   *Isaiah 29—30*
THE CHOICE: REBELLION OR TRUST

Discussion 6   *Isaiah 31—35*
WHO WILL DELIVER JERUSALEM?

Discussion 7   *Isaiah 36—39*
HEZEKIAH

Discussion 8   *Isaiah 40—45*
DELIVERANCE

Discussion 9 *Isaiah 46—48*
THE FALL OF BABYLON

Discussion 10 *Isaiah 49—53*
SERVANT OF THE LORD

Discussion 11 *Isaiah 54—59*
SEEK THE LORD WHILE HE MAY BE FOUND

Discussion 12 *Isaiah 60—63*
PROCLAIM LIBERTY TO THE CAPTIVES

Discussion 13 *Isaiah 64—66*
JUDGMENT AND HOPE

What Should Our Group Study Next?

HOW TO USE THIS DISCUSSION GUIDE

This study, Isaiah, is intended for use by adult groups who have studied a number of books of the Bible using guides in the Neighborhood Bible Studies series, and for church groups in which most members are familiar with the Bible.

Church school teachers will find Isaiah to be a study that will interest their adult classes. The guide questions are intended for everyone to use in preparation and for the leader (teacher) to use to develop thoughtful discussion during the class session. Because of the length of the material, it may be necessary to divide most of the studies if a full hour is not available for discussion.

The Book of Isaiah contains difficult sections, but you will find much to challenge and encourage you if you take time to assimilate his message into your thinking. If possible, use at least two or three Bible translations in your study.

This study guide uses the inductive approach to Bible study. *It will help you discover for yourself what the Bible says.* It will not give you prepackaged answers. *People remember most what they discover for themselves and what they express in their own words.* The study guide provides three kinds of questions:

1. What does the passage say? What are the facts?
2. What is the meaning of these facts?
3. How does this passage apply to your life?

- Observe the facts carefully before you interpret the meaning of your observations. Then apply the truths you have discovered to life today. Resist the temptation to skip the fact questions since we are not as observant as we think. Find the facts quickly so you can spend more time on their meaning and application.

- *The purpose of Bible study is not just to know more Bible truths but to apply them.* Allow these truths to make a difference in how you think and act, in your attitudes and relationships, in the quality and direction of your life.

- Each discussion requires about one hour. Decide on the amount of time to add for socializing and prayer.

- *Share the leadership.* If a different person is the moderator or question-asker each week, interest grows and members feel the group belongs to everyone. The Bible is the authority in the group, not the question-asker.

- When a group grows to more than ten, the quiet people become quieter. Plan to grow and multiply. You can meet as two groups in the same house or begin another group so that more people can participate and benefit.

TOOLS FOR AN EFFECTIVE BIBLE STUDY

1. A study guide for each person in the group.

2. A modern translation of the Bible such as:
   NEW INTERNATIONAL VERSION (NIV)
   TODAY'S ENGLISH VERSION (TEV)
   THE JERUSALEM BIBLE (JB)
   THE LIVING BIBLE (TLB)
   NEW ENGLISH BIBLE (REB)
   REVISED STANDARD VERSION (NRSV)

3. An English dictionary.

4. A map of the Lands of the Bible in a Bible or in the study guide.

5. Your conviction that the Bible is worth studying.

GUIDELINES FOR AN EFFECTIVE STUDY

1. Stick to the passage under discussion.

2. Avoid tangents. If the subject is not addressed in the passage, put it on hold until after the study.

3. Let the Bible speak for itself. Do not quote other authorities or rewrite it to say what you want it to say.

4. Apply the passage personally and honestly.

5. Listen to one another to sharpen your insights.

6. Prepare by reading the Bible passage and thinking through the questions during the week.

7. Begin and end on time.

HELPS FOR THE QUESTION-ASKER

1. Prepare by reading the passage several times, using different translations if possible. Ask for God's help in understanding it. Consider how the questions might be answered. Observe which questions can be answered quickly and which may require more time.

2. Begin on time.

3. Lead the group in opening prayer or ask someone ahead of time to do so. Don't take anyone by surprise.

4. Ask for a different volunteer to read each Bible section. Read the question. Wait for an answer. Rephrase the question if necessary. Resist the temptation to answer the question yourself. Move to the next question. Skip questions already answered by the discussion.

5. Encourage everyone to participate. Ask the group, "What do the rest of you think?" "What else could be added?"

6. Receive all answers warmly. If needed, ask, "In which verse did you find that?" "How does that fit with verse...?"

7. If a tangent arises, ask, "Do we find the answer to that here?" Or suggest, "Let's write that down and look for the information as we go along."

8. Discourage members who are too talkative by saying, "When I read the next question, let's hear from someone who hasn't spoken yet today."

9. Use the summary questions to bring the study to a conclusion on time.

10. Close the study with prayer.

11. Decide on one person to be the host and another person to ask the questions at the next discussion.

INTRODUCTION

HISTORICAL BACKGROUND:

The prophet Isaiah lived in Jerusalem in the southern kingdom of Judah during the second half of the eighth century before Christ, a pivotal period in that nation's history. King Uzziah's death in 740 B.C. came at the end of fifty years of quiet in the Middle East. During the remainder of the century, successive Assyrian kings intent on expanding their empire dealt quickly and drastically with any sign of opposition from small kingdoms on their borders. Between 734 and 722 B.C., Assyria conquered the neighboring northern kingdom of Israel. They deported many of its people and brought in settlers from other parts of the Assyrian Empire until the area lost its Israelite character and became a cosmopolitan Assyrian province.

AUTHOR:

Until the past two centuries the sixty-six chapters of Isaiah were regarded by all scholars as the work of the eighth century prophet Isaiah. The whole book was written on a single scroll, and New Testament references assume its unity. For a brief discussion of single authorship and multiple authorship, see pages 589-591 of the introduction to Isaiah in the *New Bible Commentary: Revised* (Grand Rapids: Eerdmans, 1970), and pages 701-702, Volume 2, *The Illustrated Bible Dictionary* Wheaton, Ill.: Tyndale House, 1980).

Literary form:

The Book of Isaiah is marked by majesty and beauty of expression, brilliant word pictures, and an amazing variety of style and range of feeling. The material is arranged to some degree in chronological order and partially according to subject matter.

Most of this book is written in poetic form. Hebrew poetry is deliberately redundant, characterized by the use of parallel thought rather than meter or rhyming sounds. In Isaiah the same idea may be expressed a second or third time in different words, new ideas may be added to the original thought, or one idea may be contrasted with another.

In studying Isaiah, keep in mind that several elements usually are included in prophetic literature of the Old Testament: (1)statements directed to the immediate situation; (2)predictions of future events of judgment and/or blessing; (3)the coming of the Messiah; (4)principles of right and wrong, applicable to Old Testament times and ours.

The New Testament quotes Isaiah over a hundred times, more than any other Old Testament book.

Chronology of events in the time of Isaiah:

- 745 Tiglath-pileser III becomes king of Assyria
- 740 Death of Uzziah, king of Judah
  Jotham becomes king
  Isaiah is called to be a prophet
- 735 Jotham dies, Ahaz becomes king of Judah
- 734 Tiglath-pileser invades Israel and Syria
  King Ahaz visits Damascus
  Mass deportation of people of Israel by Assyria

727	Shalmaneser replaces Tiglath-pileser as ruler over Assyria
725	Hezekiah succeeds Ahaz as king of Judah
722	Sargon II succeeds Shalmaneser as ruler of Assyria
	After three-year siege, Samaria, capital of Israel, falls to Assyria
	Remaining population of Israel deported
711	Sargon invades Syria, captures Ashdod
705	Sargon is murdered
	Sennacherib becomes king of Assyria
701	Sennacherib invades Judah, besieges Jerusalem
687	Manasseh succeeds Hezekiah as king of Judah

OUTLINE OF ISAIAH:

Chapters

1-4	Warnings of judgment	⎫
6	Isaiah's call to be a prophet	⎪
7-12	Assyria's threats and God's promises	⎪
13-23	Messages for different nations	⎬ **Prophetic**
24-27	God's final victory over all enemies	⎪
28-31	Warnings to Israel and to Judah	⎪
32-35	Deliverance	⎭
36-39	Crisis situations: King Hezekiah and Isaiah	⎬ **Historical**
40-55	Deliverance from Babylon is coming	⎫ **Prophetic**
56-66	Condemnation, rescue, future glory	⎭

DISCUSSION 1

Called To Serve

ISAIAH 6—8

In your preparation for this discussion, read chapters 1—5 aloud, visualizing the vivid word pictures the prophet uses to describe God's rebellious people. Then study chapters 6—8, using the questions provided for discussion.

At the start of your discussion session, ask one or two people to read aloud the following introduction:

In the first five chapters of Isaiah, the prophet has indicted Israel, the people of God, as rebellious sons who are utterly estranged from their Father. He has described the nation as a battered body whose wounds are untreated and the once faithful and righteous Jerusalem as a prostitute. God's vineyard, Judah, has produced only the sour wild grapes of murder and injustice.

The LORD hates and rejects the religious festivals and sacrifices which mask his people's dissolute, cynical lives. He vows to remove the very framework of their unjust society and to lay waste their proud and wealthy land. In his anger, the LORD will bring another nation to take away his people, just as snarling lions seize their prey and carry it off.

Isaiah 6:1-13
"Here I am! Send me."

1. As you read this section, try to visualize the scene Isaiah describes. In verses 1-5, what does he see? What does he hear?

Note: Verse 1, **temple**—*the holy place in front of the Holy of Holies Verse 2,* **flaming creatures** *(TEV)—heavenly beings mentioned in Scripture only in this verse. Verse 4,* **smoke**—*this recalls the scene in the temple at its dedication in the time of King Solomon (2 Chronicles 5:13-14; 7:1-13), and the scene on Mount Sinai at the giving of the Law to Moses (Exodus 19:18-20).*

2. What effect does this vision of the holiness and the glory of God have upon Isaiah?

    Of what is Isaiah keenly aware?

3. How is Isaiah's guilt removed and his sin forgiven?

Note: The one **burning coal** *represents the temple altar from which it came—that sin's penalty was paid by a substitute offered in the sinner's place.*

4. What is Isaiah's immediate response to the LORD'S question?

    What assignment is he given?

15/ Called to Serve

5. In contrast to Isaiah's awareness and confession of sin at the revelation of God's holiness, what will be the response of *this people* to the message he brings from God (verses 9-10)?

Note: Isaiah is not to expect success. The people's long continued rebellion against God has brought them to the place where Isaiah's message (which could save them if they would obey it) will only serve to harden their hearts further.

6. What is God's terrible answer to Isaiah's question in verse 11?

How complete will be his judgment of the land?

What is the one ray of hope in the picture of the burned tree in verse 13?

ISAIAH 7:1-25
A SIGN

7. King Rezin of Syria and King Pekah of Israel come to fight against Jerusalem since Judah has refused to form an alliance with them against Assyria.

What is the reaction of King Ahaz and the people of Judah to their approach (verses 2, 4)?

8. What commands from the LORD is Isaiah to give to Ahaz?

   What does God say will come of the plans of Syria and Israel (Ephraim)?

   What prediction is made about Israel's not-too-distant future?

9. Describe the exchange between the LORD and King Ahaz (verses 10-17).

   What does God want, and how does Ahaz respond?

   What is the LORD'S reaction (verse 13)?

10. What does Ahaz reveal about himself by his refusal of God's offer to choose a sign?

    What sign (verses 14-16) does the LORD himself proceed to offer the king as a guarantee of the fulfillment of his promises in verses 5-7?

Note: This sign of Immanuel and deliverance in the immediate future also concerned the then-distant future coming of Messiah. See Matthew 1:22-23.

11. What two graphic metaphors (verses 18-20) does the LORD use to describe the effects of the armies he will call to invade Israel?

Afterward, what will the land be like (verses 21-25)?

Note: Verse 15, **curds and honey**—*the meager fare of the poor.*

ISAIAH 8:1-15
ASSYRIA WILL SWEEP OVER JUDAH

12. Another more specific sign of the coming destruction of Syria and Israel is given through Isaiah. Before Isaiah and his wife conceive a son, his name, meaning **Quick pickings—Easy prey** (J. B. Phillips' translation) and foretelling disaster, is announced before witnesses at God's command.

In verse 4, what reveals how short the time is before Assyria will plunder the capitals of Syria and Israel?

13. How will Assyria's invasion of Syria and Israel affect Judah (verses 5-8)?

What contrast does God draw between his help, rejected by Judah, and the consequences of any Assyrian intervention that Judah might seek for protection from Syria and Israel?

*Note: Verse 6, **the waters of Shiloah**—God's quiet help. Verse 7, **the River**—the Euphrates (Assyria).*

14. Conspiracy (verse 12) can also be translated *treaty* and refer to an alliance. If so, Isaiah is saying, "Don't trust Assyria, or fear Syria." Instead, of whom should they be in awe (verses 11-13)?

Whom or what do people fear today?

What difference should Isaiah's vision (6:1-5) make as to whom and what you fear?

15. What does the LORD hosts (the LORD Almighty) become to those such as Israel end Judah who refuse to fear him (verses 14-15)?

ISAIAH 8:16-22
WHOM TO CONSULT

16. As the people of Judah have rejected his spoken message, what will Isaiah do (verses 16-17)?

What are the prophet and his children to be (verse 18)?

If people won't listen to God and his testimony, whom are they tempted to **consult** (RSV) NW) and **ask for messages** (TEV)?

19/ CALLED TO SERVE

What decisive advice does Isaiah give in such a situation?

17. What is the result for those who look for guidance and search for answers in the wrong way and in the wrong place (verses 21-22)?

Summary

1. Contrast Isaiah's experience in 6:1-8 with that of the people in 8:21-22.

2. What do these chapters reveal about
the call of Isaiah?

his assignment from God?

his attitude toward God?

the situation he faced as God's messenger?

3. What have you learned in these chapters about obeying and trusting God?

PRAYER

Sing or recite, as your prayer, this hymn by Reginald Heber (1783-1826):
> *Holy, holy, holy! though the darkness hide Thee,*
> *Though the eye of sinful man Thy glory may not see,*
> *Only Thou art holy; there is none beside Thee*
> *Perfect in power, in love, and purity. Amen.*

MEMORIZE

Then I heard the voice of the LORD saying, "Whom shall I send? Who will be our messenger? I answered, "Here I am. Send me." (Isaiah 6:8, JB)

DISCUSSION 2

Warnings and Joyous Promises

ISAIAH 9—12

Those living in Judah in Isaiah's time are under the threat of destruction. The prophet writes to give such people hope and courage and to challenge them to put their trust in the LORD, not in alliances with other nations.

(In your preparation for this discussion, read all of chapters 9—12 before studying the sections for which there are guide questions.)

ISAIAH 9:1-7
IN THE LATTER TIME

1. Within months after Isaiah's meeting with King Ahaz (chapter 7, about 735 B.C.), the land of the northern tribes of Zebulun and Naphtali in Israel fell to Assyria. In this prophecy, what changes are promised for them?

2. What reasons are there to rejoice?

   What has come to an end (verses 3-5)?

   What has begun (verses 6-7)? See also Luke 1:31-33.

3. What do you know about the promised ruler from the four titles in verse 6?

What will characterize his reign?

What is the source of his power?

Isaiah 9:8—10:4

The Anger of the Lord

Ask different persons to read these sections aloud: 9:8-12a 13-17a, 18-21a: 10:1-4a Have the whole group as a chorus recite verses 12b, 17b, 21b, and 10:4b at appropriate places in the reading. (Note: a or b in a verse reference designates the first or second half of that verse.)

4. Against whom has the LORD sent his message?

How would you describe their attitude (verses 9-10)?

What is the LORD's response (verses 11-12)?

5. Since the people have not repented or returned to the LORD in what additional ways will he express his anger toward Israel (verses 14-15)?

6. In verses 16-17, what do you discover about the people of Israel and about their leaders?

What happens to a church or Christian ministry which has at its head someone who confuses or misleads people?

7. As you listen to the language used in our society today, what does it reveal about our hearts (verse 17)? See also James 3:8-10.

8. Describe what the wickedness of leaders and people does to the whole society in verses 18-21. Note that Isaiah sees their self-inflicted judgment as God's judgment (verses 17, 19 21b)

9. In addition to the civil unrest in which people prey on one another (9:14-21), what characterizes the society of Israel (10:1-2)?

What does the LORD say to those who have legalized the unjust actions of their government?

10. What wrongs today are similar to those the prophet speaks against?

Who are *the poor, the needy, the widows, the fatherless* in our society?

Compare the priorities revealed by government spending with the actual needs of people in our country, in other countries.

11. Compare the attitude in Israel expressed here with the attitude that Jesus encounters in the synagogue in Mark 3:1-6.

Isaiah 10:5-34

Though God is using Assyrian armies as a tool to bring his judgment upon Israel end Judah, he will judge Assyria also for its pride. His anger against Judah will come to an end. Judah will live, but Assyria will be destroyed.

Isaiah 11:1—12:6
FROM THE STUMP OF JESSE

12. List everything you discover about the Person mentioned in 11:1-5. From what dynasty does he come (verse 1)?

What qualities will characterize him and his reign?

Who is the source of his wisdom and power?

*Note: 11:1, **the stump of Jesse** (RSV, NIV)—**the royal line of David** (TEV) 11:10, **the Root of Jesse** (NIV)—**the new King from the royal line of David** (TEV) Jesse was the father of King David.*

25/ WARNINGS AND JOYOUS PROMISES

13. What illustrations does the prophet use (verses 6-9) to describe an earth that is *full of the knowledge of the* **LORD**?

What changes will occur because of his rule (verses 4-5, 9)?

14. Share your ideas of what the world would be like if verse 9 were fulfilled. What drastic changes would have to take place?

How can we help to fulfill verse 9b?

15. From verses 10-12, 15-16, describe the return of the scattered people of Judah and Ephraim (Israel).

Who will bring them?

How and from where will they come?

16. What changed attitude will Israel and Judah have toward one another (verse 13)?

17. What freedoms does the song of chapter 12 celebrate in verse 1?

verse 2?

verse 3?

Compare 12:1 with 9:12b, 21b 10:4.

18. What do you learn about God from the witness of his people in verses 4-6?

SUMMARY

1. Contrast the attitudes of the returned survivors in the song of 12:1-6 with those of the people in 6:10; 8:21; 9:9, 17.

What will God accomplish in his people through their desolation and exile?

2. Compare the character and accomplishments of the promised Ruler of 9:6-7; 11:1-5, with those of the rulers of Israel in 9:15-16; 10:1-2.

3. What warnings should we heed from chapters 9-12?

4. What can we do specifically to obey the exhortations of 12:4-6?

Prayer

As part of your closing prayer, read this ancient hymn praising Jesus Christ, the Deliverer predicted by Isaiah:

> *Of the Father's love begotten*
> *   Ere the worlds began to be,*
> *He is Alpha, He is Omega,*
> *He the source, the ending He,*
> *Of the things that are, that have been,*
> *And that future years will be,*
> *   Evermore and evermore. Amen.*

Aurelius Clemens Prudentius (348-410)

Memorize

There shall come forth a shoot from the stump of Jesse, and a branch shall grow out of his roots. And the spirit of the LORD shall rest upon him, the spirit of wisdom and understanding, the spirit of counsel and might, the spirit of knowledge and fear of the LORD. (Isaiah 11:1-2, RSV)

SUMMARY OF ISAIAH CHAPTERS 13—23

(Even though chapters 13—23 are not included in the sections for discussion, read through them in your own personal study. Note the graphic word pictures Isaiah uses in the poetry of these oracles or messages from the LORD.)

This section of Isaiah proclaims the LORD as Ruler of the world, not only of Israel and Judah. These chapters contain prophecies of judgment against Babylon, Philistia, Moab, Syria, Israel, Cush (the Sudan), Ethiopia, Egypt, Edom, and Arabia. The LORD'S judgments of nations related to Judah will result in the ultimate deliverance of his people.

Chapter 22 concerns Jerusalem, **the Valley of Vision**, from which the prophet speaks. Egypt, on whom Judah relied for help, has been defeated, and the armies of Assyria are at the gates. Instead of repenting and calling on the LORD for help, Jerusalem prepares for siege and says, "Let us eat and drink, for tomorrow we die!"

Chapter 23 concerns the prophesied destruction of Tyre whose commercial empire covered the known world of Isaiah's day.

DISCUSSION 3

Punishment and Praise, Promise of Victory

ISAIAH 24—27

Isaiah moves from oracles concerning separate nations to predicted judgments on the whole earth. In all of these judgments, however, the deliverance and salvation of the people of God are secure.

(In your preparation for this discussion, read all of chapters 24—27 before studying the individual chapters.)

ISAIAH 24
THE EARTH MOURNS

1. What devastation will happen to the earth and its people (verses 1, 3)?

   How will this come about?

   How does verse 2 make it clear that no one will escape this catastrophe and that money won't buy a person's way out?

2. Read verses 4-5 in at least three translations. Consider this description of the earth in light of what we see happening today to our soil, air, lakes, and oceans. What

is the inevitable result (verse 6) of the actions of earth's inhabitants in verse 5?

3. What problems are described in verses 6-13?

Instead of happiness, well-being, and safety, what characterizes the *earth*, its *inhabitants,* the *city*?

4. Contrast the glimpse of future joy (verses 14-16a) with the details of present judgment (verses 16b-20).

5. How does Isaiah emphasize that there is no way of escape from the calamities predicted (verses 17-19)?

6. Who comes under judgment in verses 21-22?

Compare verse 21, *the powers above* (TEV), *the powers in the heavens above* (NIV), with Ephesians 6:12.

What glory will replace the light of moon and sun?

Compare verse 23 with Revelation 21:22-26.

ISAIAH 25
DEATH IS DESTROYED

7. List all of God's actions that Isaiah mentions in his hymn of praise (verses 1-5).

What is the response to God of those named in verses 3-5?

8. Describe the banquet (verses 6-8) the LORD of hosts will hold in Jerusalem during his reign.

What seems to be the *covering* or *veil* that will be removed (verses 7-8)?

Compare with 1 Corinthians 15:42, 54.

Note: Verse 7, **shroud, sheet** *(NIV),* **cloud of sorrow** *(TEV)* **on this mountain** *(NIV),* **on Mount Zion** *(TEV).*

9. What realization comes to the people in verse 9?

What is their response to all that God has done?

Describe your reaction to verses 7-8.

10. As an example of the LORD'S treatment of the proud, what picture does Isaiah use to describe his judgment of Moab (verses 10-12)?

ISAIAH 26:1—27:1
PERFECT PEACE

11. In this song that is to be sung in Judah, why is the city described as *strong* (verses 1-4)?

In contrast, what happens to *the lofty city* of verse 5?

12. What is the secret of serenity in times of turmoil (verses 3-4, 7-9)?

If there has been a situation in which you have experienced such peace, describe it briefly.

13. List in three columns what you observe in verses 12-19 about the identity and actions of the LORD, the actions and situation of others, and the actions and situation of the people of Judah.

Summarize briefly what you have discovered.

33/ PUNISHMENT AND PRAISE, PROMISE OF VICTORY

14. Read 25:2; 26:5, 14, 20-21; 27:1. What are God's people invited to do while he brings his wrath upon the wicked?

*Note: 27:1, **Leviathan**—probably Judah's enemies, the nations of Assyria, Babylon, and Egypt.*

Isaiah 27
The Great Trumpet

15. In verses 2-6, how is the LORD'S care for his people described?

Contrast the vineyard (verses 3-6) with its description in 5:1-6.

*Note: Verse 4, **the briers and thorns**—the enemies of God's people, who will be destroyed unless they too come and make peace with the LORD (verse 5).*

16. What different types of music might you use as a background for verse 1, verses 2-3, verses 4-5, verse 6?

If you prefer to express these verses in painting or sculpture, what medium, colors, and illustrations would you use?

17. What purpose does God seek to accomplish by the hardships and exile of his people (verses 8-9)?

*Note: **Asherah poles** (NIV), **Asherim** (RSV), **incense altars** (NIV, RSV)—carved wooden poles and stone altars used for idol worship.*

18. What is the condition of the fortified city of Israel's enemies after God's judgment?

    How are these enemies described (verse 11b)?

19. What will result from the LORD'S *threshing* of his people Israel's enemies (verses 12-13)?

SUMMARY

If you were to make a graph or a line chart of chapters 24—27, what verses would be the high point of each chapter?

Why?

PRAYER

> *God moves in a mysterious way*
> *His wonders to perform;*
> *He plants His footsteps in the sea,*
> *And rides upon the storm.*

Deep in unfathomable mines
Of never failing skill,
He treasures up His bright designs,
And works His sovereign will. Amen.

William Cowper (1731-1800)

MEMORIZE

Thou dost keep him in perfect peace, whose mind is stayed on thee, because he trusts in thee. (Isaiah 26:3, RSV)

DISCUSSION 4

Proud Crown Or Crown of Glory

ISAIAH 28

Chapters 28—33 contain a series of addresses by the prophet warning Judah against the policy of seeking help from Egypt. Chapter 28 is addressed to the rulers of Jerusalem. Its setting is the restless period of intrigue with Egypt that leads to Hezekiah's revolt against Assyria and the consequent Assyrian threat to Jerusalem of 701 B.C. (described in chapters 36—37).

(Before you discuss chapter 28, read it aloud by these sections: verses 1-4; 5-6; 7-10; 11-13; 14-17a; 17b-21; 22; 23-29.)

ISAIAH 28:1-8
PRIEST AND PROPHET

1. To what communities today might the descriptions in verse 1 apply?

   What would travel posters likely say about such a place?

   In contrast, what might its daily newspaper reveal?

2. What will happen to the **haughty crown of Ephraim's drunkards** (verse 1, JB) to bring it to the situation described in verses 3-4?

What word-pictures does Isaiah use to show the swiftness, violence, and completeness of the coming destruction?

Note: Samaria, the wealthy capital of the northern kingdom of Israel (Ephraim), was situated on a hill in the midst of a fertile valley.

3. Who is described in verses 5-6?

What will he be, and to whom?

How are his qualities in verse 6 needed by the very people to whom Isaiah speaks?

4. What happens when people in positions of spiritual leadership, or those responsible for administering justice, behave like the priests and prophets in verses 7-8?

Note: The description here is so vivid, it may describe an actual encounter between Isaiah and a group of Judah's spiritual leaders.

ISAIAH 28:9-13
THEY WOULD NOT LISTEN

5. Read verses 9-13 in the JB and TEV Verses 9 and 10 are the people of Judah's contemptuous answer to the prophet. J. B. Phillips translates verse 10 as, **Do we have to learn that the law is the law is the law, the rule is the rule is the rule?** What is Isaiah's response in verses 11-13?

   Who will be the LORD'S spokesmen to those who refuse to listen to his words through Isaiah?

   What effect will these spokesmen have on Judah?

ISAIAH 28:14-22
A COVENANT WITH DEATH

6. How does Isaiah describe Judah's rulers as he proclaims to them the word of the LORD?

   What is God's estimate of their boasts?

   On what does he see they are depending for safety (verse 15) in their alliance with Egypt and treaty with Samaria

   What might be some contemporary ways of expressing their philosophy?

7. Instead of the lies and deceit on which Jerusalem's rulers arrogantly base their confidence, how does the LORD describe the foundation and cornerstone he is placing in Zion (verses 16-17)?

What will happen to the agreements on which they base their security?

8. How is the coming disaster described (verses 17-20)?

What does verse 20 say about their resources?

9. How is the LORD'S work in verse 21 described?

Note: **at Mount Perazim**—*where the LORD enabled David to defeat the Philistine after he became king of Israel and Judah (2 Samuel 5:17-20, 25).* **Valley of Gibeon**—*the LORD gave the Amorites over to Israel's army and destroyed the fleeing Amorites by large hailstones Joshua 10:10-12a). The tragedy is that the LORD will fight against Judah instead of fighting against the enemies of his people as in the past.*

10. What will happen if Jerusalem's rulers laugh at Isaiah's warnings (verse 22)?

Isaiah 28:23-29
COUNSEL FROM THE LORD

11. Note how Isaiah uses the methods and work of a skilled farmer as a parable.

In what different ways does the farmer handle the soil?

What methods and places does he use for sowing different seeds?

What ways of harvesting are used appropriate to different seeds?

12. How does this parable illustrate God's dealings in judgment with his people Judah?

What does it show about God's actions that at first sight may seem random, capricious, or even cruel?

13. How does the farmer's wisdom contrast with that of the people to whom Isaiah is preaching?

Why is it important that the rulers of Judah listen to the wisdom and counsel the LORD gives them through his prophet?

Summary

1. If you found Isaiah 28 as a portion of an ancient scroll, what would you conclude from it about the people of Judah? about the character and power of their God?

2. *This message, too, comes from the LORD of Hosts, whose purposes are wonderful and his power great* (verse 29, NEB). What have you learned from this chapter about the power and purposes of God?

   How ought this to affect how you live your life?

Prayer

Dear LORD and Father of mankind,
Forgive our foolish ways!
Reclothe us in our rightful mind;
In purer lives Thy service find,
In deeper reverence, praise. Amen.

John Greenleaf Whittier (1807-1892)

Memorize

In that day the LORD of hosts will be a crown of glory, and a diadem of beauty, to the remnant of his people; and a spirit of justice to him who sits in judgment, and strength to those who turn back the battle at the gate. (Isaiah 28:5-6, RSV)

DISCUSSION 5

The Choice: Rebellion Or Trust

ISAIAH 29—30

"The only vice that cannot be forgiven is hypocrisy. The repentance of a hypocrite is itself hypocrisy" (William Hazlitt). Isaiah pronounces woe upon the people of Judah who are guilty of this sin. If the words of our lips are not consistent with the motives of our hearts, the LORD will not accept even our most eloquent prayers.

(In your preparation for this discussion, read through chapters 29—30 before studying the individual sections)

ISAIAH 29:1-14
INCONSISTENCY

1. Contrast the situation described in verses 1-4 with the promises of verses 5-7.

   What is going to happen to ***Ariel?***

   Then what will happen to their enemies?

*Note: Verse 2, **she shall be to me like an Ariel** (RSV)—Ariel can be translated "the hearth of God." The city of Jerusalem would* *be like a fireplace hearth on which the fire of God's judgment is kindled.*

2. Note carefully all the comparisons made in verses 5-8.

3. What contrasts are drawn between the invasion by Jerusalem's foes and the actions of God (verses 5-6)?

What will happen to their plans to conquer Jerusalem (verses 7-8)?

Note: This promise was partially fulfilled in 701 B.C. See 37:33-37.

4. Instead of responding with trust and joy to these promises of the LORD'S deliverance, what will be Jerusalem's reaction to Isaiah's message (verses 9-12)?

5. What happens to a people (verses 11-12) when their spiritual leaders (***prophets, seers***) are blindfolded and sound asleep (verse 10)?

6. In some churches today, the Bible is like the ***sealed scroll*** (TEV) of verse 11. What steps can you suggest that will open the Bible to the people in such churches?

7. Describe the worship of ***this people*** (verse 13) as the LORD sees it.

What will he do because of this (verse 14)?

8. Consider your own church. To what extent, if any, does verse 13 describe it?

   What traditions might be reviewed and changed in order to make the life of your church more vibrant?

Isaiah 29:15-24
Fresh Joy

9. Describe the actions and attitudes of the people in verse 15.

   What does the prophet have to say to them (verses 15-16)?

   What have they forgotten about the relationship between them selves and God?

   Compare verse 16 and Genesis 2:7.

10. List the changes foretold in verses 17-24.

11. Instead of the attitudes depicted in verses 13-15, what will characterize the house of Jacob (Israel) in verses 23-24?

Share an experience you have had in acquiring spiritual instruction and understanding.

Isaiah 30:1-7
A Poor Choice

This message is delivered as envoys from King Hezekiah are leaving Judah for Egypt to ask the Pharaoh's help against the Assyrians (703-702 B.C.).

12. How does the LORD regard these people, and their plans to form an alliance with Egypt?

What are the pitfalls of such an alliance?

What will come of it?

13. How may this passage be a warning to us in a situation where we are tempted to collaborate with those whose objectives are not consistent with our highest spiritual values and goals?

Isaiah 30:8-18
A Witness Forever

14. Against what kind of people is Isaiah's written message to be a lasting witness?

How do verses 10 and 11 illustrate their attitudes toward *the LORD'S instruction* (verse 9)?

What do they want instead of the message God is sending them?

15. Ask one person to review the people's attitude in verses 9-11. Have another group member read God's response (verses 12-14).

16. What will result from their sin of rejecting the Holy One of Israel and relying on the lies of Egypt for protection?

With what pictures does God describe the peril facing Judah?

17. Instead of repentance and rest, quietness and trust in the LORD, what do the people choose to depend on?

What will be the result (verses 15-17)?

Compare this with Deuteronomy 32:30. What similar responses have you observed today?

18. In spite of the people's rejection and rebellion, what does the LORD desire to do for them (verse 18)?

ISAIAH 30:19-33
"THIS IS THE WAY, WALK IN IT"

19. Sum up the words of encouragement in verses 19-33. What will happen to Jerusalem's enemies, the Assyrians?

Share an experience in which you sensed that you were being guided. See verse 21.

20. How do you think that Isaiah would express verse 22 today?

To what do we need to say, **Begone!** (RSV), **Away with you!** (REV)?

SUMMARY

1. What possible explanation do you find in 30:9-12 for the spiritual blindness described in 29:9-12?

What explanation is there in 29:19 for the spiritual alertness in 29:18?

2. What do these chapters reveal about:
    the foolish choices made by Judah?

    their consequences, spiritual and physical?

    the desires and purposes of God?

PRAYER

Immortal, invisible, God only wise,
In light inaccessible hid from our eyes,
Most blessed, most glorious, the Ancient of Days,
Almighty, victorious, Thy great name we praise. Amen

                      Walter Chalmers Smith (1824-1908)

MEMORIZE

For thus said the LORD GOD, the Holy One of Israel, "In returning and rest you shall be saved; in quietness and in trust shall be your strength." (Isaiah 30:15, RSV)

DISCUSSION 6

Who Will Deliver Jerusalem

ISAIAH 31—35

Many products today have warning labels attached to the package. These chapters contain warnings, political and personal, but there are also promises of great joy to come.

(In your preparation, read through chapters 31—35 before starting to study the sections chosen for discussion.)

ISAIAH 31
STUMBLING HELPERS

1. On whose help has Judah refused to depend by sending to Egypt for help against Assyria?

   How does Isaiah show the foolishness of their choice?

2. What principle can you draw from Isaiah's message that might apply to decisions about international alliances and political intrigue today?

3. What do the pictures of the **great lion** and **birds hovering** show about the LORD and his care for Jerusalem (Mount Zion)?

What does he promise to do (verses 4-5)?

4. What two actions does Isaiah call for in verses 6-7?

   What do you think the LORD would command his people to *reject* if Isaiah were his spokesman today?

5. Compare Isaiah's prediction concerning Assyria (verses 8-9) with what happens to the invader in 37:36-37.

ISAIAH 32
A KING WILL REIGN IN RIGHTEOUSNESS

6. Describe the character of the future **king**, his **princes** and people in verses 1-5, 8.

   What, do you think, would society be like in this kingdom?

7. Note the similarity between the description in verse 2 and how the LORD GOD is depicted in 25:4 and 26:4.

8. Contrast the people in verses 3-5 with those in 30:10-11; 29:9-10.

9. What practices in verses 6-7, all too common and accepted in our society today, will be unacceptable in the coming kingdom that Isaiah describes?

10. As Isaiah turns to the immediate future, what change of conditions will the careless women of Jerusalem face (verses 9-14)?

11. When *the Spirit is poured upon us from on high*, what will happen to the land and its people (verses 15-20)?

What effects will *righteousness* (verse 17) have?

If peace is lacking in a home, community, or nation, what may be the cause?

ISAIAH 33—The Assyrian hordes have destroyed the northern kingdom of Israel. Judah has paid an enormous tribute to secure the promise that Jerusalem will be spared, but Assyria breaks the treaty and lays siege to the city.

ISAIAH 33:1-9
A PLEA FOR HELP

12. What does Isaiah say will happen to the traitorous enemy (verse 1)?

13. How is the plight of Judah end Jerusalem described (verses 7-9)?

In that situation, what does Isaiah do (verses 2-6)?

What confidence does he express?

14. Read verses 7-9 in TEV. What political situation today does it aptly describe?

ISAIAH 33:10-24
GOOD NEWS FOR THE UPRIGHT

15. What will be the effects on the enemy of the LORD'S intervention (verses 10-13)?

On the people of Zion (verses 13-14)?

16. What is God's answer to his people's question (verses 15-16)?

17. In verses 17-24, instead of arrogant tribute collectors and foreign soldiers, what will the people of Jerusalem see when the LORD delivers the city?

What will be the cause of this serenity (verses 21-22)?

What will be the condition of Jerusalem and its people?

Note: Verse 21—the picture of a city protected by waters no hostile fleet can use; verse 23a—the disarray of the lawless invader.

ISAIAH 34—This chapter describes God's judgment on the nations of the world and on Edom in particular.

ISAIAH 35
CHEER UP! GOOD NEWS

18. What do the changes in nature in verses 1-2 reflect?

Describe an experience you have had of seeing God's glory and majesty reflected in nature.

19. In what situation have you tried to encourage a friend in deep distress with words similar to verses 3-4?

When God comes to save, what are the results described in verses 5-10?

Compare verses 5-6 with Matthew 11:2-6.

SUMMARY

1. List the LORD'S names and the ways he is described (31:1-2, 4-5; 33:5-6, 14, 21-22; 35:2, 4).

2. Describe the changes in attitude and actions the LORD desires in his people (31:6-7; 32:1-5; 33:13-16).

3. When the LORD delivers his people, what will happen to their enemies (31:3, 8-9; 33:1; 34:2-13)?

In contrast, how will God's deliverance affect his people (32:15-20; 33:5-6, 17, 20, 24; 35:1-10)?

PRAYER

When all Thy mercies, O my God, my rising soul surveys,
Transported with the view, I'm lost in wonder, love, and praise.
Through every period of my life Thy goodness I'll pursue;
And after death, in distant worlds, the glorious theme renew.
Through all eternity to Thee a joyful song I'll raise;
But O! eternity's too short to utter all thy praise. Amen

Joseph Addison (1672-1719)

MEMORIZE

And a highway shall be there, and it shall be called the Holy Way; the unclean shall not pass over it, and fools shall not err therein... But the redeemed shall walk there. And the ransomed of the LORD shall return, and come to Zion with singing; everlasting joy shall be upon their heads; they shall obtain joy and gladness, and sorrow and sighing shall flee away. (Isaiah 35:8-10, RSV)

DISCUSSION 7

Hezekiah

ISAIAH 36—39

The sequence of events recorded in these chapters is arranged for literary effect, not in order of occurrence. Hezekiah's illness and recovery and the visit of Babylon's envoys (chapters 38—39) take place before the Assyrian invasion and retreat (chapters 36—37).

Assyria has been the dominant world power, the threat on the horizon. It's defeat (predicted by Isaiah in chapters 8, 10, 30) makes a fitting conclusion to chapters 1—35. Chapters 38—39 form an introduction to chapters 40—66, in which Babylon is the world power, and the prophecies relate to Judah's exile and captivity in Babylon.

(In your preparation for this discussion, read through chapters 36—39 before studying the individual chapters.)

ISAIAH 36
A BROKEN REED

1. Imagine that you are to make a dramatic documentary film of this chapter. Describe briefly the groups and individuals involved, the sequence of events, and their location.

Note: 2 Kings 18:17 mentions three Assyrian officials; hence the delegation of three representatives sent by Hezekiah to meet them.

2. Ask someone in the group to forcefully read the Assyrian official's speech in verses 4-10.

   What do you think would be the emotions of Hezekiah's delegation and of the people on the wall listening to this encounter?

3. What is the Assyrian's line of argument in verses 4-7?

   Compare his accurate comment on Egypt with the LORD'S words through Isaiah in 30:3, 7.

   Yet, how has the official either misunderstood or perhaps deliberately misinterpreted Hezekiah's reforms?

   Compare verse 7 with 2 Kings 18:3-6

4. What wager does the Assyrian offer in verse 8 to taunt Judah? Note how he uses the report he seems to have heard that Assyria's invasion is a punishment from the LORD.

   Compare 36 10 with Isaiah's prophecies in 10: 5-6; 7:17-20.

5. The Judean officers try to keep Assyria's threats from being understood by those who could overhear the negotiations. What happens to frustrate their attempt?

6. What does the Assyrian repeatedly urge in his speech to all who can hear him (verses 13-20)?

   How does he cleverly seek to undermine their confidence in King Hezekiah?

7. What is the fallacy in his reasoning in verses 18-20?

   What is the wisdom in Hezekiah's command to keep silent?

   What have you learned in your own experience about the wisdom of silence?

8. What does the action of Eliakim, Shebna, and Joah (verse 22) indicate about their evaluation of the situation?

Isaiah 37
Hezekiah's Prayer

9. What three actions does Hezekiah take immediately upon hearing the report of his men?

How does the king view the situation (verses 3, 4)?

What is his request to Isaiah?

10. What message from the LORD does Isaiah send to Hezekiah? Summarize it in your own words.

How is the promise of verse 7 soon fulfilled?

11. Describe the letter from the Assyrian emperor, Sennacherib (verses 10-13).

How would you feel if you received a similar message in a time of difficulty?

What "gods" are failing people today?

12. How does Hezekiah respond to Sennacherib's letter? Look carefully at each part of his prayer:
    How does Hezekiah address God?

What does he believe about God?

How does he view Sennacherib's words?

What difference does Hezekiah recognize between *the* **LORD** *our* **GOD** and the gods of the nations destroyed by Assyria?

With what request does he conclude his prayer?

13. How is King Hezekiah's prayer answered?

What is the LORD'S reply to Sennacherib's threats (verses 22-29)?

How does God view the Assyrian's boastful words and actions?

What will happen to Sennacherib (verses 28-29, 33-34)?

to Jerusalem (verses 30-32, 35)?

14. What happens to the Assyrian and to Sennacherib?

Note: There was an interval of some twenty years between the events of verses 36-37 and those in verse 38.

ISAIAH 38
A SIGN FROM THE LORD

15. What word from the LORD does Isaiah bring to the desperately ill Hezekiah?

Describe the king's reaction and the LORD'S very specific response through Isaiah (verses 4-8, 22).

Note: Verse 8, **the shadow cast by the sun... on the stairway of Ahaz.** *Stairs as well as sundials were used to show time. There is no indication in the text how the LORD'S sign is accomplished—perhaps a change in the refraction of rays.*

16. In Hezekiah poetry about his illness and recovery, how does he describe:

    his reactions to the approach of death (verses 10-11)?

    the finality of death (verse 12)?

    the pain and weakness of his illness (verses 13-14)?

    the benefits derived from the experience (verses 15-20)?

Isaiah 39
Showing the Treasures

17. Describe Hezekiah's response to the envoys who bring letters and a gift from the king of Babylon.

18. How does Isaiah evaluate what this visit and Hezekiah's response to it would mean in coming days?

Note: The real reason behind the visit probably is Babylon's desire to secure Hezekiah's support and to form an alliance against the Assyrians. To the Babylonian envoys, Hezekiah's display of his treasures would be a temptation to conquer Jerusalem and seize its wealth.

Summary

1. Review briefly the sequence of events in chapters 38 and 39.

What does King Hezekiah's learn about the LORD that would help him to face the threat of invasion by Assyria (recorded in chapters 36-37)?

2. In chapters 36-37, what do you learn from Hezekiah's actions and prayer about how to handle desperate situations in your life?

PRAYER

"Our hope is in no other save in Thee;
Our faith is built upon Thy promise free;
LORD, give us peace, and make us calm and sure,
That in Thy strength we evermore endure. " Amen.

John Calvin (1509-1564)

MEMORIZE

And Hezekiah prayed to the LORD: "O LORD Almighty, God of Israel, enthroned between the cherubim, you alone are God over all the kingdoms of the earth. You have made heaven and earth. Give ear, O LORD, and hear; open your eyes, O LORD, and see... O LORD our God, deliver us... so that all kingdoms on earth may know that you alone, O LORD, are God." (Isaiah 37:15-17, 20, NIV)

DISCUSSION 8

Deliverance

ISAIAH 40—45

Chapter 40 opens on the far side of the disaster which Isaiah predicted in 39:5-8. The prophet's message now is directed to the people of Judah, captives in Babylon since the fall of Jerusalem in 587 B.C., who are nearing the end of their long captivity.

(In preparing this study read through chapters 40—45 before studying the chapters for which there are discussion questions. You may wish to handle this discussion in two sessions.)

ISAIAH 40
GOOD NEWS

1. What wonderful news does God have for his people (verses 1-5)?

   How is their predicted return home described?

   Who will lead the procession and who will watch it?

2. To what is the brevity of human life compared?

With what is it contrasted (verses 6-8)?

3. Ask two people to act as announcers. Have one person read verse 9 from the NIV, or RSV, and the other from the TEV or TLB.

From verses 10-31, list all the things you discover about God.

4. How is God's relationship to his people described in verses 11, 29-31?

What is your response to such a God?

Isaiah 41
Deliverance

The prophet predicts a conqueror from the north and east (verses 2, 25) who will terrify the nations, but God promises protection and deliverance for his people. He addresses Israel as his servant (verses 8-10) and promises that his people, now crushed and beaten (verse 14), will again by his help have an impact on the world.

ISAIAH 42:1-9
GOD'S SERVANT

This is the first in a series of five songs describing the servant of the LORD.

5. What do you learn about God's *servant*, his *chosen one*?

What will he do?

What will he not do?

For the fulfillment of this passage in Jesus, compare with Matthew 12:9-21; Luke 2:27-32; 4:14-19; 7:20-23.

6. How is God the LORD described in verses 5-9?

For whom is he concerned?

ISAIAH 42:10-25
A NEW SONG

7. Who is to join in singing the *new song* of praise to the LORD(verses 10-12)?

*Note: Verse 11, **Kedar** and **Sela** (the chief town of Edom)—Israel's bitter rivals last mentioned in terms of judgment in 21:16-17 and 34:5ff*

8. The LORD is described as a warrior and as a woman in labor whose time has come to deliver. What will the LORD do to his enemies (verses 13, 15, 17)?

In contrast, how will he treat his people?

9. How is God's servant, Israel, described in verses 18-20, 24b?

What does the LORD want his people to recognize about what has happened to them (verses 22-25)?

(If you wish to discuss this study in two sessions, plan to divide it at this point).

ISAIAH 43:1-7
FEAR NOT

10. In spite of Israel's spiritual blindness and deafness, what promises does the LORD make to his people in exile?

What reasons does he give for his concern (verses 1, 4, 7)?

ISAIAH 43:8-13
GOD ALONE KNOWS THE FUTURE

11. Read this section aloud from the TEV. The setting is an imaginary courtroom. ***The nations*** are summoned to attend, and the ***people of Israel*** are called as God's witnesses. What is the issue to be heard (verses 9-10)?

    What does the past history of Israel reveal about the LORD (verses 10-13)?

ISAIAH 43:14-28
ESCAPE FROM BABYLON

12. How will the LORD deliver his people from captivity (verses 14-21)?

    In what ways will this deliverance (verses 19-20) differ from their exodus from Egypt centuries before?

13. What indictment does God bring against his people ***Israel*** (verses 22-28)?

    What have they done, and what have they failed to do?

    In spite of all this, what gracious promise does the LORD give to them (verse 25)?

Isaiah 44:1-23
"Listen, Israel, Whom I have Chosen"

Addressing his servant Israel as chosen and beloved, the LORD promises spiritual power and blessing to his people whom he has forgiven (in 43:25). He reminds them that there is no other god, and it is he alone who predicted all that has come to pass. After a scathing description of the stupidity of making and worshiping idols, the LORD reminds Israel of his saving grace.

Isaiah 44:24—45:13
Cyrus, My Shepherd

14. How does the LORD describe himself and his activities?

What does he predict concerning its temple, and Judah?

15. What is Cyrus to do as the LORD'S *shepherd* and his *anointed* one?

What will the LORD do for Cyrus even though Cyrus does not *acknowledge (know)* him?

16. What reasons does the LORD give for using Cyrus (45:6, 13)?

What is God's answer to anyone who may question his actions (verses 9-12)?

69/Deliverance

Isaiah 45:14-25
Turn to Me and Be Saved

The LORD returns to the courtroom scene and calls people of all nations to acknowledge him as the only God, ***a righteous God and a Savior before whom every knee shall bow, by whom every tongue shall swear*** (RSV).

Summary

1. List all the names and activities of God from chapters 40—45.

2. If you were asked to be on a debating team and given the topic "God's superiority over idols," what arguments from these chapters would you use to win your debate?

Prayer

LORD of all being, throned afar,
  Thy glory flames from sun and star;
Center and soul of every sphere,
  Yet to each loving bears bow near!
Grant us Thy truth to make us free,
  And kindling heart that burn for Thee;
Till all Thy living altars claim
  One holy light, one heavenly flame. Amen.

              Oliver Wendell Holmes (1809-1894)

MEMORIZE

Have you not known? Have you not heard? The LORD is the everlasting God, the Creator of the ends of the earth He does not faint or grow weary, his understanding is unsearchable. He gives power to the faint, and to him who has no might be increases strength (Isaiah 40:28-31, RSV)

DISCUSSION 9

The Fall of Babylon

ISAIAH 46—48

Not only will Cyrus conquer Babylon and its empire, but he will send its captives home, proving that the LORD does control and predict the course of history. The prophet continues his efforts to turn the exiles of Israel away from idolatry and turn them toward dependence upon God, the Creator of the universe, who has called Israel to be his servant.

(In preparing for this discussion, read through chapters 46—48 before you begin to study each chapter.)

ISAIAH 46
IDOLS

1. What will happen to the gods of Babylon?

   What reveals their helplessness?

   In our culture, what gods do people serve today?

   What evidence have you observed of their failure to strengthen and deliver their worshipers?

*Note: Verse 1, **Bel**—the title given to Marduk, Babylon's patron deity, whose son **Nebo** was the god of learning.*

2. What contrasts does the LORD draw between himself (verses 3-4) and Babylon's helpless idols (verses 1-2, 6-7)?

   Dr. G. Campbell Morgan writes: "An idol is a thing which man makes and has to carry. The true God makes a man and carries him."

3. Note the commands the LORD gives his people in verses 3, 8-9, 12. What is the attitude of these captives?

   What is your response to God as you see him revealed in this chapter?

4. What purpose will the LORD accomplish? How?

ISAIAH 47:1-15
SORCERIES AND DESTRUCTION

5. What drastic changes will come to Babylon?

   What will happen to the **Virgin Daughter of Babylon, queen of kingdoms** (NIV)?

Note: This dirge, or taunt-song, against the ruthless Babylonian Empire pictures a haughty queen humbled to the posit ion of a menial slave. Verse 2, **wade through the streams**—*probably refers to going into exile.*

6. For what attitudes and actions is Babylon being judged so harshly (verses 6-10)?

7. On what does Babylon depend for security (verses 9b, 12-13)?

   In what similar things do people trust today?

   What warning does this chapter have for those who trust in anything or anyone other than God?

8. When Babylon's destruction comes, what will happen to her astrologers and their predictions (verses 14-15)?

ISAIAH 48
"LISTEN TO ME, ISRAEL"

9. Read verse 17, and then list the commands in verses 1a. 12a, 14a, 16a. One can picture a parent or schoolmaster speaking these words to a group of rebellious children.

   Compare the response of earth and sky in verse 13b to what God wants of Israel in verse 14a.

10. Compare the words which the **house of Jacob** (*people of Israel*) speaks (verses 1-2) with their inner attitudes (verses 4, 8) and their trust in idols (verse 5). How would you describe these exiles?

11. What reasons does God give for the disasters his people have experienced? Note that he does not let them be destroyed.

12. What reasons does the LORD give for long ago predicting future events and then bringing them to pass (verses 3-6a)?

13. What **new things** (verse 6b) is the LORD announcing before they take place? See 46:11, 13; 47:1, 9, 13; 48:14b-15, 20.

14. Compare verses 18 and 22. In contrast to suffering deportation and exile, what would have happened to Israel if only they had listened to God and obeyed his commands (verses 18-19)?

15. What two responsibilities have those who are set free by Cyrus (verses 20-21)?

How does this new exodus remind the people of their escape from Egypt under Moses' leadership?

16. What is the warning to those who reject God's promises of deliverance (verse 22)?

SUMMARY

1. Describe the exiles from Israel as they are shown in chapters 46—48.

2. How are the patience and love of God revealed in these chapters?

   How is his power revealed?

3. What contrasts are drawn between the LORD and the idols of Babylon?

PRAYER

Lead us, heavenly Father, lead us
  O'er the world's tempestuous sea;
Guard us, guide us, keep us, feed us,
  For we have no help but Thee;
Yet possessing every blessing,
  If our God our Father be. Amen.

James Edmeston (1791-1867)

Memorize

O that you had hearkened to my commandments! Then your peace would have been like a river, and your righteousness like waves of the sea. (Isaiah 48:18, RSV)

DISCUSSION 10

Servant of the Lord

ISAIAH 49—53

Chapters 40—48 reveal the LORD'S superiority over the gods of the nations. The destruction of Babylon is predicted and the opportunity for Israel's exiles to return home. In the next section (chapters 49—57), redemption is promised for the whole world through the Servant of the LORD.

(In your preparation for this discussion, read through chapters 49—53 before studying the sections for which there are guide questions. You may wish to handle this study in two sessions.)

ISAIAH 49
"REJOICE, O EARTH"

1. To whom does the LORD'S servant address his message?

   What do you learn about his call to be a servant and his preparation (verses 1-3, 5)?

   From the phrases **like a sharpened sword** and **a polished arrow**, what will God use his servant to do?

   What is God's purpose (verses 3, 5)?

2. When nothing comes of the efforts of the LORD'S servant, what is his attitude (verse 4)?

   How may this verse help you in your daily struggles?

3. What greater task does God have for his servant to do?

   Compare verse 6 with Luke 2:27-32 and Acts 26:23.

*Note: This is the second of Isaiah's five servant songs. In these songs, the **servant** seems to personify Israel in three ways: the nation as a whole, its people chosen of God to be his messenger to all the world; the righteous remnant within Israel which seeks to bring the rebellious nation back to God to be a witness for him among the nations; a Person, the Messiah, who embodies the noblest qualities and ideals of the people of Israel.*

4. What transformation is promised for Israel in exile (verses 7-13)?

   List the specific actions the LORD promises to take in verses 8-11.

5. To those who believe that he has forgotten his people, what does the LORD answer (verses 14-16)?

   What arrival and departure will take place (verses 18-21)?

6. Jerusalem is to be rebuilt and its population restored. How will this come about (verses 22-26)?

What will *all mankind* know as a result of God's actions on behalf of his people?

What encouragement do the promises in verses 15 and 23c offer to you?

Isaiah 50
An Instructed Tongue, A Listening Ear

7. What is the LORD'S answer to those who think that there is an irreparable breach between him and his people?

To those who think that he lacks the power to rescue them (verses 1-2, RSV)?

8. Describe the LORD'S servant as he is revealed in this third servant song (verses 4-9).

What is his relationship to the *Sovereign* **LORD** (NIV, TEV), **LORD** *God* (RSV)?

What confidence does this give him?

80/ISAIAH

9. How does the LORD'S servant act toward those who reject him and his message?

Compare verse 6 with Matthew 26:65-67; 27:26b-31.

10. What encouragement and what warning for yourself do you see in verses 10-11?

Isaiah 51
"Look! Listen! Lift Up Your Eyes!"

The prophet calls the people of God to remember how the LORD brought their nation into being from one childless couple, Abraham and Sarah. To his fearful people God promises righteousness and justice, and salvation that lasts forever. They are to return to Jerusalem with gladness, for his anger against them is over. God's wrath will now be turned against those who have tormented his people.

Isaiah 52:1-12
"The Lord Will Go Before You"

11. In verses 1-2, what are God's people told to take off? to put on?

Rephrase verse 2 in your own words.

81/SERVANT OF THE LORD

12. Of what events in their history does the LORD remind them in verses 3-6?

What important fact should they be aware of (verse 6b)?

Note: Verse 3, **you were sold for nothing** *(NIV)—Israel's captors have no claim against Israel or God. They are only agents of God's judgment, and he does not owe them anything.*

13. Describe in detail how you would make a film of the events in verses 7-12.

What do you see?

What do you hear?

How are the departing captives protected (verse 12)?

What are they to bring with them (verse 11)?

When are you aware of needing special protection?

In what circumstances have you experienced the LORD protection?

(If you wish to discuss this study in two sessions, plan to divide it at this point.)

ISAIAH 52:13-53:12
"WOUNDED FOR OUR TRANSGRESSIONS"
Artists since the first century AD. have tried to capture a likeness of the person described in this section. This is the fourth in the series of servant songs. As you read it, look for parallels in the life and death of Jesus Christ.

14. Read 52:13-15 in the TEV, NIV, and RSV. Describe *my servant* and what happens to him in the past and in the future.

15. What effect will the suffering and death of the LORD'S servant have on *many nations* and their rulers?

16. Read 53:1-6 in the NIV and TEV. Notice that this section is spoken in the first person (*we, ours, us*), and most of it is in the past tense.

How is the LORD'S *servant* described here?

17. What do people fail to recognize (verses 1-3)?

What treatment does the LORD'S servant receive?

Compare Matthew 27:27-44.

83/SERVANT OF THE LORD

18. In contrast to what *we* thought of the LORD'S servant (verse 4), why did he suffer (verses 4-6)?

What did he accomplish by his suffering?

19. List all the things about *us* that made his suffering necessary.

20. What facts does Isaiah mention that fit the events surrounding Jesus' death?

Compare verses 7-9 with Matthew 27:11-14, 19-26, 57-60, and 1 Peter 2:21-23.

21. Read verses 10-12 in the JB and TEV. What explanation is given for the suffering and death of God's servant?

Note his willingness (verse 12).

Compare this with the explanation for Jesus' death given in Hebrews 2:9-10, and 1 Peter 2:24-25.

SUMMARY

1. Describe God's attitudes toward his people Israel, his commands to them, and what he promises to do for them.

2. From these chapters, summarize what you have discovered about the servant of the LORD, God's purposes for him, what happens to him, and his accomplishments.

PRAYER

"Man of Sorrows," what a name
For the Son of God who came
Ruined sinners to reclaim!
Hallelujah! What a Savior!

Bearing shame and scoffing rude,
In my place condemned He stood;
Sealed my pardon with His blood;
Hallelujahs! What a Savior!

Philipp Bliss (1838-76)

MEMORIZE

All we like sheep have gone astray; we have turned every one to his own way; and the LORD has laid on him the iniquity of us all. (Isaiah 53:6, RSV)

DISCUSSION 11

Seek the Lord While He May be Found

ISAIAH 54—59

Isaiah continues his prophecies of restoration, inviting the people to turn to God and to worship him in integrity and righteousness.

(In your preparation for this discussion, read through chapters 54—59 before you begin to study the chapters for which discussion questions are provided.)

ISAIAH 54
COMPASSION

Here Isaiah addresses the Jewish nation as a wife whose husband is the LORD and as a city whose foundations and walls are jewels and precious stones. Jerusalem, seen during the Babylonian captivity as a childless widow, is told to enlarge her dwelling to accommodate all the children she will have. The LORD affirms his everlasting love to his people and his covenant of peace with them. They are to be taught and defended by the LORD Almighty, made strong by righteousness, freed from tyranny, fear, and terror.

ISAIAH 55:1-56:8
SEEK THE LORD

1. What urgent invitation does God give to his people in exile (55:1-2)?

How are they described?

What actions does the LORD urge people to take?

What will be the result?

2. If what we *eat* (verse 2) includes everything we take in (books, films, television, music), are we eating what is *good*, what will truly *satisfy*? If not, why not?

3. What does the LORD promise to his people who *listen* and *come* to him (verses 3-5)?

*Note: Verse 3 see Psalm 89:20-29 for God's **covenant** and his **steadfast, sure love for David** (RSV).*

4. Read verses 6-7, in the NIV, JB, and TEV. List the immediate actions urged in these verses.

   What is God's response to those who accept his invitation?

5. What reasons are given as to why the repentance called for in verses 6-7 is necessary (verses 8-9)?

What contrast is drawn between the ways and thoughts of God and the ways and thoughts of human beings?

6. To what is the *word* of the LORD compared in its effects and its effectiveness (verses 10-11)?

7. What will the LORD accomplish for his exiled people?

   How would you express verses 12 and 13 in song, dance, or painting?

8. Describe times when nature has reminded you of God's power and presence. What expression in nature of God's love and power has been most impressive to you?

ISAIAH 56:1-8
"A HOUSE OF PRAYER FOR ALL NATIONS"

9. What actions toward him and toward one another does the LORD command of his people in exile (verses 1-2)?

   Why?

10. How do the *foreigners* (non-Jews) who had joined themselves to Israel express their feelings of unworthiness (verse 3)?

What does the LORD require of them, and what is their reward (verses 4-7)?

For Jesus' use of verses 7-8, see Matthew 21:12-13 end John 10:16.

11. What is the LORD'S message to the *eunuchs* who fear God but who wonder if they will participate in the promised deliverance (verses 5b-8)?

How does God's promise sensitively answer their handicap?

Note: See Deuteronomy 23:1. The law against emasculation protested such heathen cultic practices and sought to prevent the introduction of this kind of mutilation in Israel.

12. Instead of physical wholeness or proper lineage, what does God consider essential for one to be a part of his people?

ISAIAH 56:9-57:13
ISRAEL'S LEADERS AND IDOLATRY CONDEMNED

This section may refer to the times of Manasseh, Hezekiah's son, who persecuted the innocent and sacrificed his own child to the idol Molech (2 Kings 21:6, 16). Israel's leaders are spiritually blind men who seek their own advantage, and the evils accompanying idol worship have filled the land. The

LORD gives a scathing indictment of his people's attitudes and actions and warns that their idols will not be able to save them from his judgment. Only those who trust in him will inherit the land and worship in his temple.

ISAIAH 57:14-58:14
THE TRUE FAST

13. In 57:14-21, Isaiah returns to his prophecy of the exiles' return from Babylon.

What is revealed about God in these verses?

List all that you learn about him, his characters and attitudes.

In spite of Israel's willfulness and sinful ways, what is God's intention for his people (verses 18-19)?

14. What do the people seem to want, but what don't they understand (58:1-5)?

15. What is wrong with their *fasting*?

Instead of bringing them into deeper fellowship with God, what does their fasting produce?

16. Describe the kind of conduct that pleases God (verses 6-10).

Why would such behavior be called *fasting*?

What will be the results (verses 10-12)?

17. Describe the kind of Sabbath-keeping that pleases God. What will be its consequences (verses 13-14)?

ISAIAH 59
SIN, CONFESSION, REDEMPTION

This chapter describes in graphic detail the sins that have separated the people from God and slowed his promised deliverance. Instead of the light, healing, and fruitfulness produced by righteousness (58:8, 10-12), their iniquity has led to darkness and stumbling.

Identifying himself with his people, the prophet confesses their sins and the degradation and distress that have resulted. Seeing that there is no one to intercede, the LORD himself acts to bring salvation. He promises a Redeemer to those who repent of their sins, and he announces an eternal covenant in which his Spirit and his words will not depart from his people

Summary

1. What does the LORD offer to people who turn away from sin and turn to him?

2. Describe briefly in your own words how one can express loyalty and honor to God and love for others in ways that please him.

Prayer

Guide me, O Thou great Jehovah,
   Pilgrim through this barren land;
I am weak, but Thou art mighty;
   Hold me with Thy powerful hand
   Bread of heaven,
Feed me till I want no more.

Open now the crystal fountain,
   Whence the healing stream cloth flow;
Let the fire and cloudy pillar
   Lead me all my journey through;
   Strong Deliverer
Be Thou still my strength and shield. Amen.

William Williams (1716-1 791)

MEMORIZE

Seek the LORD while he may be found, call upon him while he is near; let the wicked forsake his way, and the unrighteous man his thoughts; let him return to the Lord, that he may have mercy on him, and to our God, for he will abundantly pardon. (Isaiah 55:6-7, RSV)

DISCUSSION 12

Proclaim Liberty to the Captives

ISAIAH 60—63

Chapter 60 is a vision of **Zion, The City of the Lord** (verse 14) after God has fulfilled all of his purposes toward her. The glory of the LORD upon the city attracts the nations and their kings, end Jerusalem's sons and daughters return from far places. The desolate forsaken city is rebuilt, its temple made beautiful. Righteous, peaceful, and strong, Zion's unfailing light is the presence of the Lord.

While the prophet certainly has in mind the return from Babylon, he uses terms of wider application which John later borrows in his description of the New Jerusalem, the Church of Christ, in Revelation 21:23-26.

(In your preparation for this discussion, read through chapters 60—63 before you study the individual chapters.)

ISAIAH 61
THE SPIRIT OF THE SOVEREIGN LORD

1. Find at least ten things in verses 1-3 that the one spoken of here is to do.

   When first spoken, how would these words apply to the deliverance from Babylon and the return to Jerusalem?

For their later fulfillment, read Luke 4:14-21. What examples can you give of Jesus Christ fulfilling verses 1-3?

2. What transformation will take place in these brokenhearted captives, and what will they accomplish (verses 3-4)?

What will now be the experience of God's people?

3. In verses 5-9, what changes will take place in the life of God's people?

Though formerly dishonored, what new reputation and ministry will they have? See also Exodus 19:5-6.

*Note: Verse 6, **priests of the Lord**—those who have access to God.*

4. What are the causes for rejoicing in verses 10-11?

Where and when have you seen such expressions of praise to the LORD?

What occasions have you had to share in worship and praise to the LORD with men and women from other nations?

Isaiah 62
No Longer Forsaken

5. What place does persistent prayer have in bringing about Jerusalem's redemption and vindication which have been promised (verses 1, 6-7)?

6. Describe the changes Isaiah predicts for God's people in verses 2-5, 10-12.

Who will witness this?

What do the name changes for Jerusalem and Judah reveal of how God feels about them?

7. Compare the rejoicing in verse 5 with that which Jesus mentions in Luke 15:7, 10.

When, do you think, does the LORD rejoice over us and delight in us?

Compare your response to God with that in 61:10.

8. What sure promises does the LORD make to his people (verses 8-9, 12)?

9. What will be the **new name** for those who return from exile?

Compare verses 2 and 12.

Isaiah 63

10. Have verses 1-3 read aloud as a dialog. Ask three people to read in unison the questions (verses 1a-2). Ask a fourth person to respond with the replies (verses 1b, 3-6). What do you learn about this warrior?

11. What does this warrior accomplish for his people?

Compare with Revelation 19:11-16, where Jesus, Son of God, is the warrior.

12. In verses 7-14, the prophet reviews the dealings of the LORD with his people Israel. Describe his attitude toward them and all his actions on their behalf in the exodus from Egypt (verses 7-9, 11-13a) and in the land of Israel (verses 13b-14).

13. What is Isaiah's prayer on behalf of his people (verses 15-19)?

On what relationship does he base this prayer?

What are his requests?

What questions does he raise?

14. What do you learn about God from verse 16?

15. Note the people's past attitude (verse 10) and their current attitude (verse 17). Verse 17 in the NEB reads: ***Why, Lord dost thou let us wander from thy ways and harden our hearts until we cease to fear thee?***

    Compare with God's words to Isaiah in 6:9-13.

SUMMARY

1. In chapters 60—63, what changes are predicted for the exiles of Israel and for Jerusalem?

   What will this mean for those who have oppressed the people of God?

2. Summarize what is revealed about God in these chapters. Note the names that he is called, his attitudes and actions.

   What is the appropriate response to such a God? Compare with your own response.

Prayer

Father of heaven, whose love profound
A ransom for our souls bath found,
Before Thy throne we sinners bend;
to us Thy pardoning love extend.

Edward Cooper (1770-1833)

Jesus, Thy blood and righteousness
My beauty are, my glorious dress;
Midst flaming worlds, in these arrayed,
With joy shall I lift up my head.

Bold shall I stand in Thy great day,
For who aught to my charge shall lay?
Fully absolved through thee I am,
From sin and fear from guilt and shame. Amen.

Nicholas Ludwig von Zinzendorf (1700-1760)

Memorize

I will greatly rejoice in the LORD my soul shall exult in my God; for he has clothed me with the garments of salvation, he has covered me with the robe of righteousness. (Isaiah 61:10, RSV)

DISCUSSION 13

Judgement and Hope

ISAIAH 64—66

In the previous chapter, after reviewing the past mercies of the LORD, Isaiah has confessed the deplorable spiritual state of his people. He has addressed the LORD as their Father, even though their ancestors Abraham and Israel Jacob) would be ashamed to acknowledge them (63:16). Isaiah's prayer continues in chapter 64.

(Read through chapters 64—66 before you study the individual chapters using the guide questions. You may wish to handle this discussion in two sessions.)

ISAIAH 64
CLAY AND POTTER

1. What does the prophet want God to do?

   What are his reasons for possibly expecting such intervention by the Lord (verses 3-5a)?

   Compare verse 3 with Exodus 19:16-19.

2. Compare verse 4 with Psalm 130. What do you think it means to *wait for* the LORD?

3. As Isaiah continues his prayer, what does he remember and what confessions does he make (verses 5b-7)?

   With what comparisons does he describe the sad and desperate state of those who continue to sin against God (verse 6)?

4. Read verse 7 in the RSV and NIV. What are the terrible results of the people's continued sinning?

5. What is the effect of the word *yet (but)* at the beginning of verse 8?

   On the basis of what relationship does Isaiah plead pardon and deliverance for his people?

6. What does Isaiah's picture of God as *potter* and his people as *clay* and *the work of his hand* reveal to you about God?

   What are some of the things a potter does with clay?

   How might these apply to us?

7. What reasons does the prophet give for his final appeal (verses 10-12)?

101/JUDGMENT AND HOPE

Phrase his questions in verse 12 as a positive request.

ISAIAH 65
JUDGEMENT AND SALVATION; NEW HEAVENS AND NEW EARTH

8. In this chapter, God answers Isaiah's prayer of 63:15-64:12. What has prevented the Lord from receiving and blessing Israel (verses 1-7)?

9. Contrast the Lords attitude and actions with those of his people in verses 1-2. Read verses 1-2, in the NIV, RSV, JB, and To or TLB.

10. Describe in contemporary terms the life-style of the people in verses 2-5, 7b, 1 lb.

What does *following their own devices* (RSV) include?

Note: The practices listed here are forms of idolatry specifically forbidden in Deuteronomy 12:2-7, 13-14; 14:3-8; 18:9-11. In verse 5a, they claim a sort of magical "holiness" from doing these things.

11. What are God's reactions to these people and their sins (verses 5-7, 12)?

12. What picture describes the few who seek God in the midst of the many who forget him (verse 8)?

What will God do for his **servants** (verses 8-16)?

Contrast the lives of those **who forsake the LORD**. What will their final outcome be (verses 12, 15)?

13. Why do those who forsake the LORD turn to the gods of **Fortune** and **Destiny** (verse 11)?

Consider how much money, time, and energy is spent on gambling (luck and fate) in our country today. What does it cost in terms of human misery?

*Note: Verse 11, **Gad** and **Meni**—the gods of luck and fate (TEV), **Fortune** and **Destiny** (NIV, RSV), were worshiped in Syria and other places.*

14. In verses 15b-25, list the many changes that will take place. What will characterize life in the **new heavens and new earth** to be enjoyed by those who obey and serve the LORD?

Note: Commentators vary in interpreting this section as to whether it pictures in figurative language Israel redeemed and restored to her land, or speaks of the final state of all things in the perfect world to come.

(If you wish to handle this study in two sessions, plan to divide it at this point.)

ISAIAH 66
TREMBLE AT GOD'S WORD

15. What titles would you give to the LORD from his description of himself in verses 1-2?

What dwelling place will please him?

16. Read verse 2 in several translations.

What attitudes does God expect and honor in his people?

Compare your own attitudes toward God with this standard.

*Note: **contrite**-literally **broken**, with no inward rebellion.*

17. How does God view the sacrifices and offerings of those who ***have chosen their own ways*** (verse 3)?

What does the LORD ***choose*** for them?

Why?

---

104 / ISAIAH

What is your response when the LORD calls and speaks?

18. What will happen to those who hate and scoff at God's faithful people (verses 5-6)?

19. Describe the picture that is drawn of **Zion** (Jerusalem) and the restored people of Israel in verses 7-11.

What details are added to the picture in verses 12-13?

20. Contrast the blessings for those who obey the LORD (verses 11-14) with his judgments on those who reject him (verses 14c-17, 24).

21. Read verses 18-21 in several different translations.

What message will be proclaimed among the nations?

What offering will be brought to the LORD from among them?

Compare Matthew 28:18-20; Acts 1:8.

22. Compare verses 22-23 with Revelation 21:1, 22-27.

SUMMARY

1. Trace the strong contrasts drawn between those who go their own way and those who respond in obedience to God in chapters 64—66.

   What characterizes their lives?

   What will be the result of their choices? Read 55:6-9.

2. In answer to the prophet's prayer (64:1, 9, 12), what blessings does the Lord promise (65:8-66:23)?

PRAYER

Give to our God immortal praise,
Mercy and truth are all His ways;
Wonders of grace to God belong,
Repeat His mercies in your song.

Give to the Lord of lords renown;
The King of kings with glory crown
His mercies ever shall endure,
When lords and kings are known no more. Amen.

Isaac Watts (1674-1748)

MEMORIZE

From of old no one has heard or perceived by the ear, no eye has seen a God besides thee, who works for those who wait for him. (Isaiah 64:4, RSV)

WHAT SHOULD OUR GROUP STUDY NEXT?

We recommend the Gospel of Mark, the fast paced narrative of Jesus' life, as the first book for people new to Bible study. Follow this with the Book of Acts to see what happens to the people introduced in Mark. Then in Genesis discover the beginnings of the world and find the answers to the big questions of where we came from and why we are here.

Our repertoire of guides allows great flexibility. For groups starting with *Lenten Studies*, *They Met Jesus* is a good sequel.

LEVEL 101: little or no previous Bible study experience

Mark *(recommended first unit of study)* or The Book of Mark *(Simplified English)*

Acts, Books 1 and 2
Genesis, Books 1 and 2
Psalms/Proverbs
Topical Studies
Conversations With Jesus
Lenten Studies
Foundations for Faith
Character Studies
They Met Jesus

> **Sequence for groups reaching people from non-Christian cultures**
> Foundations for Faith
> Genesis, Books 1 and 2
> Mark, Discover Jesus *or* The Book of Mark *(Simplified English)*

LEVEL 201: some experience in Bible study (after 3-4 Level 101 books)

John, Books 1 and 2
Romans
I John/James
1 Corinthians
2 Corinthians
Philippians
Colossians
Topical Studies
Prayer

Treasures
Relationships
Servants of the Lord
Change
Work – God's Gift
Celebrate
Character Studies
Four Men of God
Lifestyles of Faith, Books 1 and 2

LEVEL 301: More experienced in Bible study

Matthew, Books 1 and 2
Galatians & Philemon
1 and 2 Peter
Hebrews
1 and 2 Thessalonians, 2 & 3 John

Topical Studies
Character Studies
David
Moses
Set Free

Isaiah
Ephesians

***Biweekly or Monthly Groups may use topical studies or character studies.*

ABOUT NEIGHBORHOOD BIBLE STUDIES

Neighborhood Bible Studies, Inc. is a leader in the field of small group Bible studies. Since 1960, NBS has pioneered the development of Bible study groups that encourage each member to participate in the leadership of the discussion.

The mission of Neighborhood Bible Studies is to: Mobilize and empower followers of Jesus Christ to introduce and multiply small group discussion Bible studies among their neighbors, co-workers, and friends so that participants can encounter God, grow in faith, and pattern their lives after Jesus.

The vision of Neighborhood Bible Studies is to: Invite people everywhere to a relationship with Christ through the study of God's word.

Publication in more than 20 languages indicates the versatility of NBS cross culturally. NBS **methods and materials** are used around the world to:

> Equip individuals for facilitating discovery Bible studies
> Serve as a resource to the church

Skilled NBS personnel provide consultation by telephone or e-mail. In some areas, they conduct workshops and seminars to train individuals, clergy, and laity in how to establish small group Bible studies in neighborhoods, churches, workplaces and specialized facilities. **Call 1-800-369-0307 to inquire about consultation or training.**

ABOUT THE FOUNDERS

Marilyn Kunz and Catherine Schell, authors of many of the NBS guides, founded Neighborhood Bible Studies and directed its work for thirty-one years. Currently other authors contribute to the series.

The cost of your study guide has been subsidized by faithful people who give generously to NBS. For more information, visit our web site: www.neighborhoodbiblestudy.org   *1-800-369-0307*

COMPLETE LISTING OF NBS STUDY GUIDES

Getting Started
How to Start a Neighborhood Bible Study *(handbook & video or audio cassette)*

Bible Book Studies
Genesis, Book 1 *Begin with God*
Genesis, Book 2 *Discover Your Roots*
Psalms & Proverbs *Journals of Wisdom*
Isaiah *God's Help Is on the Way*
Matthew, Book 1 *God's Promise Kept*
Matthew, Book 2 *God's Purpose Fulfilled*
Mark *Discover Jesus*
Luke *Good News and Great Joy*
John, Book 1 *Explore Faith and Understand Life*
John, Book 2 *Believe and Live*
Acts, Book 1 *The Holy Spirit Transforms Lives*
Acts, Book 2 *Amazing Journeys with God*
Romans *A Reasoned Faith*
1 Corinthians *Finding Answers to Life's Questions*
2 Corinthians *The Power of Weakness*
Galatians & Philemon *Fully Accepted by God*
Ephesians *Living in God's Family*
Philippians *A Message of Encouragement*
Colossians *Staying Focused on Truth*
1 & 2 Thessalonians, 2 & 3 John, Jude *The Coming of the LORD*
Hebrews *Access to God*
1 & 2 Peter *Strength Amidst Stress*
1 John & James *Faith that Lives*

Topical Studies
Celebrate *Reasons for Hurrahs*
Conversations with Jesus *Getting to Know Him*
Change *Facing the Unexpected*
Foundations for Faith *The Basics for Knowing God*
Lenten Studies *Life Defeats Death*
Prayer *Communicating with God*
Relationships *Connect to Others: God's Plan*
Servants of the LORD *Embrace God's Agenda*
Set Free *Leaving Negative Emotions Behind*
Treasures *Discover God's Riches*
Work - God's Gift *Life-Changing Choices*

Character Studies
Four Men of God *Unlikely Leaders*
Lifestyles of Faith, Book One *Choosing to Trust God*
Lifestyles of Faith, Book Two *Choosing to Obey God*
They Met Jesus *Life-Changing Encounters*
David *Passion Pursued*
Moses *Learning to Lead*

Simplified English
The Book of Mark *The Story of Jesus*

NOTES

Notes